MW01170402

NO
REGRETS!

Living Your Life to the Fullest

BY
DR. GABRIEL E.
WARREN

Warren
Publishing Group

Birmingham, AL

To my awesome wife, Ebony, and to our beautiful son, Gabriel, II. I love you both with all my heart, and look forward to us living life with no regrets.

ACKNOWLEDGEMENTS

First and foremost, I thank God who is my strength, encouragement, and source of empowerment. To my beautiful wife, Ebony, I appreciate the love and support you show me in everything I set out to do. Your resilience and prayers are felt as I do God's will. I thank you for giving me the space to be the "me" God has called me to be. I love you so much!

Bishop L. Spenser and Lady Patrice Smith, words alone cannot express the level of wisdom and insight your lives have given me. It is an honor to sit under you as spiritual parents. I undoubtedly know that without you allowing God to use you to minister the Gospel so effectively, I would not be the person I am today. Your works are impacting lives forever. I appreciate everything you do.

To my mother and father, A.V. and Clementine Warren, thank you for raising me and teaching me the principles of Christ, and the work ethic it takes to live a life that is pleasing to God. I am grateful for everything you have done to push me into my destiny. Thank you for sacrificing the little you had, so that I could press forward and have a fulfilling life. I am so happy that God chose me to be your son. To my brothers: Andrae, Joshua, and Joseph, and sisters: Cynthia and Bernadette, I love you. Thank you for your continued support.

Ronald and Mary Hunter, thank you for believing in me, and trusting me with the precious gift of your daughter. You continuously amaze me by the level of love you always show toward me. I thank God for the genuine people you are in my life.

Howard and Marilyn Speights, you guys are definitely a blessing. The sound wisdom and guidance you share with Ebony and I are irreplaceable. Thank you for showing us how to live a life of freedom and abundance in Christ. You will always be cherished in our hearts.

Galvin and LaTosha Billups, we love you guys! For everything you have done for us, we just say thank you. We look forward to celebrating a life long friendship with you.

Darius Foster, thank you for taking the time to help me grow. The knowledge gained through our relationship was vital to this book being completed.

Marilyn Young, thank you for everything you've done to make this book possible. Without your diligence, I would not have been able to complete it on time.

Thank you to everyone who has had a hand in shaping the person I have become. The many prayers, tears, financial contributions, and encouraging words you gave has helped fuel the writing of this book. Without you, none of this would ever be possible! You are appreciated and will never be forgotten!

No Regrets! by Dr. Gabriel E. Warren
Published by Warren Publishing Group,
a division of GE WarrenSpeaks
P. O. Box 361391
Birmingham, AL 35236
www.gabrielewarren.com
www.facebook.com/DrGabrielWarren

All Scripture quotations are from the KJV Prophecy
Marked Reference Study Bible. Copyright © 1998 by
the Zondervan Corporation.

Cover Design and page layout by Ebony T. Warren.
Photo taken by Demetrius Foy of Dfoy Photography,
Birmingham, AL

Printed in the United States of America.

ISBN-10: 0-615-22600-0
ISBN-13: 978-0-615-22600-2

CONTENTS

	Introduction	11
1.	Daily Confessions	15
2.	Daily Quite Time	21
3.	Desire to be Different	27
4.	Building Winning Relationships	33
5.	Prayer Life	39
6.	Being Mentored	45
7.	Expect the Unexpected	51
8.	Formulate a Plan	57
9.	Read, Read, Read	63
10.	Overcoming Fear	69
11.	In Conclusion	75
	About the Author	79

INTRODUCTION

I always wondered what it would take for someone ordinary to write a book. Did I have to get a degree in English or Journalism? How long would it take to compile the information I needed before writing the book? Is what I have to say valuable enough for others to read? Similar types of questions run through our minds as we embark on something new in life. Although, some people are displeased with where their lives have ended up thus far, fear prevents them from believing in the impossible and doing something different.

Life means more than just living one day at a time. Many joyous occasions make life meaningful, like having a new husband or wife, a new baby, or a new job. If a person feels no joy or satisfaction on the inside, these things may seem minute, but not for me. For this reason, I found myself fighting to write this book, not because it was hard for me to do, but because I know that somewhere out there, someone needs this book.

As you read the following pages, I pray your life is enlightened. I also pray that your passion will be stirred again, because I know how the issues of life can have a way of weighing down your dreams. Therefore, I must warn you that this book is NOT for you if you think your life is too bad for change to happen. It also isn't for you if you have decided to give up and not strive to become successful. For everyone else, enjoy the ride as I enlighten and encourage you on your path to living your life to the fullest with NO REGRETS.

1 Chapter One

DAILY CONFESSIONS

Proverbs 23:7 states "For as he [man] thinketh in his heart, so is he..." I've come to the realization that this is an absolute must in order for you to be successful in life. There has to be some form of personal confession that comes out of your mouth on a daily basis. It doesn't matter whether it's rehearsed on the way to work, or standing in front of the mirror. I was once told that if you want something bad enough, you will eat, sleep and breathe whatever you desire.

The power of professing and speaking things into the atmosphere is such a powerful thing. Every successful person you come in contact with will tell you that they had to constantly confess what they wanted their lives to look like until it looked like what they confessed. When your life doesn't look how you desire it to look, the first thing you must do is change your mindset to think like what you are trying to become. The very next thing you have to do is begin to speak into existence the life you want to have. The Bible instructs us to speak those things that be not as though they were (Romans 4:17).

Growing up in a family of eight, there were times when I felt as if life required me to go to school, work hard making someone else rich, and then retire at age 65. I know I wasn't the only one raised this way. Most people in similar circumstances never experience generational wealth for themselves or their families. Because of this simple truth, I learned not to allow my external circumstances to create a reality for me. That's when I decided to confess that I would do something great, and live my life outside the box of status quo.

This mentality caused me to be the first child in my family to make the junior high basketball team and continue to play throughout high school, while competing in two other sports and maintaining a part-time job. Also, I was able to remain an "A" student throughout high school, graduating in the top 15 percent of my graduating class with a GPA of 3.85.

Making daily confessions also afforded me the opportunity to be the first person in my family to get a scholarship to a major Division I university as a student-athlete in track & field. From there, I went on to be the first sibling to get my bachelor's degree from a major university, while competing in athletics and earning All-SEC Honor Roll recognition. One year after graduation, I decided to start my own marketing and graphic design company and the following year I published my own magazine, and started a publishing company.

These accomplishments would have never been possible if I didn't take the time to realize there was a different life for me. Take a moment and think about how you see your life now, and then take a few more minutes to think about how you want your life to be. What are some thoughts that come to your mind? Write them down and think about the life you desire. I encourage you to make a conscious effort to recite your confessions at least twice a day, once in the morning and once before bedtime. Then you will begin to see how your way of thinking will totally begin to change.

2 Chapter Two

DAILY QUIET TIME

Taking time out to meditate on godly things will make you a better person. Philippians 4:8 says, "Finally, brethren, whatsoever things are true, whatsoever things are honest, whatsoever things are just, whatsoever things are pure, whatsoever things are lovely, whatsoever things are of good report; if there be any virtue, and if there be any praise, think on these things."

While pursuing your destiny, you may find yourself alone. These critical moments you spend with God and with yourself will bring forth opportunities for individual growth. When you meditate, you actually slow down your day, and you're able to think things through and avoid having to make decisions on the run. However, there will be times when you're not able to sit and have personal reflections, but strive for at least 30 minutes a day.

In your quite time, you should make it a point to rehearse your entire day's activities in your mind. See yourself going into that job interview and getting hired on the spot. Picture yourself walking into the bank with a flawless business plan and getting the loan to finance your company. Imagine yourself making the best sales presentation. Whatever you want to pursue that day, you must know that success is a possibility for you.

Some people may find themselves afraid to be quiet for a period of time. Some may be afraid of the unknown, but on the other side of the unknown is the life you've always dreamed about. Sometimes being afraid is the fuel that helps you get through the uncertainty of not knowing. Ask yourself, if God were to show you everything it was going to take to get you to your destiny, would you still be a willing participant? Being disciplined to have a daily quiet time also opens you up to look at things differently. New ideas, strategies, and visions are all birthed out of daily quiet time.

On your journey of pursuing your destiny, you must make time to meditate and strategize about the direction you should take your life, and the decisions you should make. The first step to take would be to sit down and schedule time for reflection each and every day. By doing this, you can begin to hold yourself accountable, making sure you abide by that standard.

Think about a time that would be most convenient for you to spend at least 30 minutes a day reflecting. Write down this time and commit to doing it everyday.

_____

_____

_____

_____

_____

_____

_____

_____

_____

_____

_____

_____

_____

_____

_____

_____

_____

3 Chapter Three

DESIRE TO BE DIFFERENT

Status quo is not acceptable! While growing up, I never desired to do things the same way others did them. In order to pursue your destiny there must come a time in your life when you must decide not to be normal. Going against the grain should become your normal way of life once you start on the path to your destiny.

There will be plenty of people who will not agree with what you choose to do, or with the way you go about doing it. If you are serious about your destiny, you must focus on your dreams, not on the opinions of spectators. Life is full of people who become comfortable with living a normal life. Change is necessary, but there will be people who will not readily agree with what you are doing. I've never met anyone who was not affected in some way by the mechanism of change. Whether you agree or not, adjusting has to take place. These are some of the things you must hold close to you.

Entrepreneurship is on the rise in our country, mainly because people are becoming tired of ordinary living. There is such a wide gap between the "haves" and the "have nots," and it's mainly because wealthy people have a desire to do something different. Having this desire is financially and emotionally rewarding. Over one-half of the wealthy people in our country became wealthy because they had the desire to implement something different. These people are able to spend more time with their families, take vacations, and even create generational wealth for their children and grandchildren. Can you imagine how satisfying it would be to know your children won't face your challenges? At some point you must ask, do I want my children to start their life where I am now? If the answer is no, then there is work to be done and changes to be made.

Each of us are born with a desire to do something extraordinary. You realize this by identifying those things you do better than most people. What do people constantly ask you about? Whatever it may be, it is a vital clue in you discovering your purpose. What hobbies do you enjoy? What do people say you're good at? These are a few questions to help you get started. I believe you have the desire to be different, because if you didn't you would not have picked up this book. Therefore, I encourage you for the next few minutes to take out a pen and write your answers to those questions. From there, think about how you can use those things to make your world a better place.

No Regrets!

_____
_____
_____
_____
_____
_____
_____
_____
_____
_____
_____
_____
_____
_____
_____
_____
_____
_____
_____
_____
_____
_____

4 Chapter Four

BUILDING WINNING RELATIONSHIPS

Your destiny being fulfilled has everything to do with knowing how to establish, maintain, and nurture your relationships. This is very important, because it will have an effect on every aspect of your life. It doesn't matter if you desire to move up the corporate ladder, start a business, or home school your children. At some given point you must rely on the relationships you have established, and there must always be a will inside of you that causes you to keep adding to your relationships.

Doors can be opened through investors, mentors, and supporters providing some of the things you will need to be successful. These types of relationships are important because the resources they can provide can save you a lot of time and money. How many times have you heard of the individual that wanted to start his own business, but it seemed impossible? Then, you found out that because of the right relationship, that individual is now a successful business person, who started the business on a small budget. If built correctly, the right relationship can propel you into your destiny with just one phone call.

I'm sure you may be familiar with the six degrees of separation principal, but if not, I'll explain. The premise behind this principal is that you can ultimately get in contact with anyone you desire if you utilize the relationships you currently possess. The people you currently know have access to relationships that can lead you to other people, who will then lead you to the person you desire to reach. Everything that will ever come to you will come through some type of relationship. Nothing happens by accident. It doesn't matter if it's a father and son, mother and daughter, or employer and employee. Your success is vitally dependant upon how you are able to maintain and nurture relationships.

Trust is a key component to any relationship. In order for someone to trust you with their resources and contacts, they must know you will not damage their reputation. We all spend a lifetime building and establishing relationships. We must be very careful how we utilize those relationships. Once someone opens the door for you, they must know you will have integrity. No one will trust you with another contact if they feel you won't live up to your fullest potential. You have to give them an opportunity to believe in you, and know you are prepared for your destiny.

Success is when opportunity and preparation intersects. The opportunity is always presented through a relationship. Preparation solely depends upon you. Always remember there's no such thing as a one man band. Every successful person has a host of relationships they stand on, and that allows them to further fulfill their destiny.

While pursuing your destiny, you must have the ability to build strong, healthy relationships. Know that this will take time and patience. Always surround yourself with positive people. If your current friends have the same things you have or less, then you must locate people on the level you are pursuing. By doing this, you give yourself the possibility of not having to go through some of the pitfalls they had to endure. Also, these people may have resources and contacts that will help you to make it to the next level in your field.

Use this time to think about the people you currently have in your circle of influence. People like your college professor, pastor, community leader, co-worker, or family member all have the ability to help connect you with other people that may be vital to your success. Write down their names and contact information in the space provided. Take time to call them and explain your vision. You'll be surprised at the response you'll get. Just remember, if someone doesn't agree with what you are doing, don't give up on your dreams.

_____

_____

_____

_____

_____

_____

_____

_____

_____

_____

_____

_____

_____

_____

_____

_____

_____

_____

_____

_____

_____

_____

_____

_____

_____

_____

_____

_____

5 Chapter Five

PRAYER LIFE

Developing and retaining a prayer life is vital. There is no way you will be able to pursue your destiny unless you have an active prayer life. Jeremiah 1:5 states, "Before I formed thee in the belly I knew thee; and before thou camest forth out of the womb I sanctified thee, and I ordained thee a prophet unto the nations." In this scripture, God reveals to Jeremiah a truth that still applies to us today. We were created and gifted to perform a specific task on earth. Every talent, skill and ability given to you is a product of God equipping you to complete your destiny.

It is imperative that you develop a personal prayer life with God, so He can lead you in the right path. Throughout your journey, you will be faced with various obstacles that will force you to rely on your inner strength. Having a prayer life gives you the strength to press forward when seemingly the world is against you.

Prayer opens up many doors that otherwise would have been shut. The power of prayer causes transactions to be made on our behalf from heaven to the earth. When we pray, we give God an opportunity to get involved with our lives and do something spectacular with us.

While in prayer, God can reveal to you things that could change your life. Million dollar ideas are created in moments of prayer. The conceptualization of successful relationships are formulated as well. Time and opportunity meets while you are praying. Prayer builds confidence in you, and creates a swagger for you to know that what you are striving to achieve will happen. After you finish praying, you can go into the world, and see the manifestation of what you unlocked in your prayer time.

When you pray, you are communicating with God, and He is waiting for you to reach out to Him. He has so much to tell you. Please know that I have prayed for God to give you all of the answers you need in order to start pursuing your destiny.

For the next few moments, take some time to ask yourself the following questions: How often do I pray? When I pray, do I give myself time to meditate and get answers? Has anything in my life been impacted because of my prayer life? Do I know the next step in pursuing my destiny? Write down your answers and ask God to help you make the proper adjustments.

No Regrets!

6 Chapter Six

BEING MENTORED

Once you have determined your goals and discovered your destiny, now you have the awesome task of finding a mentor to train you in that field. There is no sense in trying to reinvent the wheel. Today everyone wants to be the ninth wonder of the world, coming up with ideas to flatter other people. Although this is an audacious effort, it can sometimes be very costly and unsuccessful. There is a reason why experience is needed. It is the thing necessary for you to have in order to avoid mistakes.

Mentors provide the opportunity for you to acquire experience in much less time than they did. Through the valuable years of up and down experiences, mentors have survived the test of time, and have proven to be viable forces in their industries.

Often times, while you are pursuing your destiny, you will come up against challenges that may seem insurmountable. It's in these very critical moments that mentorship shows its value. Mentors can pour into you and motivate you. Most times they have been in the same situation and are overcomers. Also, mentors possess a wealth of key relationships in the industry that can prove to be important to your success.

Unlike most of your peers, mentors have an ability to see your potential, and challenge you to become a better person. Instead of them flattering your every decision and telling you how wonderful they think you are, they constantly point out the areas in which you could be stronger.

Think about the relationship of a head coach with his basketball team. One of the ways you can tell the difference between a good coach and a great coach is by looking at his ability to develop a great player. Someone can be a good player, and it is the job of the coach to identify his weak areas, so that player can become one of the best in the game. If no one ever challenges the player to be better, then he will never meet his optimal potential. This is the role a mentor should play in your life.

A mentor should be someone who has first proven to be successful in your desired industry. They should be able to challenge you, and force you to succeed. Mentors cause you to think things through before ever making a decision. They can make you think about problems that could arise that you never would have seen. You must be able to value the opinion of your mentor. If your mentor tells you to do something and you don't do it, then you have to check whether or not you respect him.

Preferably, your mentor should be someone of the same sex as you. This aids in helping you to stay focused on the reason you want him or her to mentor you. You must be willing to make the investment and allow someone to help you. Most of the time, this means you may have to do work and not get paid for it. At this point in the game you are more interested in gaining the wisdom, knowledge, and relationships needed. Therefore, do not get caught up in the money right off.

Use this time to write down your potential picks for mentors, and why you chose him or her.

_____

_____

_____

_____

_____

_____

_____

_____

_____

_____

_____

_____

_____

_____

_____

7 Chapter Seven

EXPECT THE
UNEXPECTED

For a brief moment, let's do an exercise. It will take about two to three minutes so get out a sheet of paper. Now, let's imagine you have just started your dream business, and your business plan is perfect. Several months of hard work is about to pay off, so now all there is to do is go to the bank to get a small business loan. Wow! You got approved. Everything is good to go. Now it's time to sit down and write out your client list. Take one minute and write down the first 10 potential clients you think you're going to have. I'll take a guess that most, if not all, of your list includes your closest friends and family. Am I right?

I decided to name this chapter "Expect the Unexpected" for a couple reasons. As entrepreneurs, we sometimes feel as if everyone we know is going to automatically support our venture. Well, they're not. Please do not think that because your friends tell you your idea will work and they support you 100 percent, that they will be the first ones to really jump on board. Most of the time, you will gain a large amount of your support by establishing relationships along your journey as an entrepreneur.

You must not expect anyone on your potential client list to be your biggest supporters. Don't get me wrong, some of them may turn out to be great supporters, and they may be with you throughout the process of becoming a successful individual, but do not solely depend on those who are familiar with you. This will keep you from feeling like you have to depend on everyone you know. There are a wealth of people who can potentially become your clients; you just have to locate them. You must be willing to get out of your comfort zone.

Not receiving the proper emotional support can be devastating for anyone who is just starting out on the road to pursuing their passion. However, there are countless testimonies from people who only had the ability to dream big when they started out on their journey. They didn't stop when no one wanted to get their autograph or call them to speak at conferences. Instead, they chose to utilize the rejection as fuel and become better.

There must be something burning inside of you that constantly pushes you to strive for your goal. You must be aware that not all of the people you associate with are going to support your business. However, they are not to blame. Most of your closest friends and family may want to, but may not know how to support you. So when it comes down to dealing with them, expect the unexpected.

For the next couple of minutes, take some time and write out the mission statement for your business. Think about why you are so passionate about the thing you want to do. What drives you? Keep this page handy, and when things get tough, take this out and get your momentum back. When you don't get the support you expect, you must encourage yourself.

_____

_____

_____

_____

_____

_____

_____

_____

_____

_____

_____

_____

_____

8 Chapter Eight

FORMULATE A PLAN

Planning is a vital step to becoming successful. When you get in your car to go on a trip where you've never been before, you have to map out directions. There's a famous saying that goes something like this, "If a person tells me what they want, I can help get them there, but the problem is getting people to tell you what they want." In other words, people don't know what it is they really want!

How many people do you know who have absolutely no idea about how they are living their lives? They wake up and move with the happenings of the day, just taking life as it comes. There is no plan or objective to get a specific task done. All they know is that they have to go to work and come home.

For most people, after this part of their day is complete, they are lost about what else to do, so they just start planning for their next day at 5 p.m. once they leave their job.

In order for you to live your life to the fullest, this mundane routine can't remain a reality for you. You must sit down and think about what you can do to make a difference in the lives of others. If your life was to end right now, outside of your immediate family, who else would be directly or indirectly affected by you not being here anymore? If you ask yourself this question and can't come up with anyone, then now is a very defining moment for your life. Today is the only thing you have the power to change, so do something with the time you have lost. Please do not sit and ponder the reality of the question I posed to the point of discouragement. Instead, allow it to ignite a fire and passion to make your life matter. Because in reality, your life does matter! If it didn't, God would have never allowed you to be placed in the earth. You are a change agent who must create change for the earth.

This is why planning is such an important factor in living a successful life. So how do you plan? The first thing to do is think about what you want to accomplish. If I asked 100 of your closest friends and family what they think your life's mission is, what would they tell me? There should be some consistency in the answer I receive. Everyone who knows you should know what you are about.

First, think about what you want to accomplish and write it down. Secondly, think of ways to fulfill your ideas. What actions are going to yield the proper results you desire? If your life's mission is to become a business owner to empower youth throughout the community and teach them how to become entrepreneurs, then you must be willing to start your business. At this point other people's lives are depending on you fulfilling your destiny.

Thirdly, you must possess a will to achieve what you desire. There will constantly be challenges and setbacks to everything you do, but your passion must override them. Your passion is the thing that will get you through until you start seeing results. Lastly, find a mentor. You must locate someone who can help you. These steps are not everything you need, but they can help you get started. I know you will find them very useful in your pursuit.

Think about your passion. Write down your life's mission and how you plan to achieve it. Plan out time frames in which you would like to get things accomplished. This will help you stay focused and organized, which will prepare you to move forward in the realization of your vision.

_____

_____

_____

_____

_____

_____

_____

_____

_____

_____

_____

_____

_____
_____
_____
_____
_____
_____
_____
_____
_____
_____
_____
_____
_____
_____
_____
_____
_____
_____
_____
_____
_____
_____

9 Chapter Nine

READ, READ, READ!

Leaders are readers. It's as simple as that. There is so much knowledge available that there's no way you will ever be able to get it all. However, there's nothing that says you can't try. We are people of habit, and the more we read, the more habits we create in our minds. This causes your thinking to change. As a leader, you must take the attitude of always wanting to learn more about your passion.

Our world is full of change. How things are today, will not be how they are tomorrow. Therefore, the power of thinking is the most valuable asset you will ever possess. Reading consistently trains our minds to think and exercise its ability to be creative. Our brains are muscles that we must build and tone up, just like every other muscle in the body. The more books you read, the more you will be able to analyze situations and come up with sound solutions. While pursuing your passion and striving for your dreams, there will be plenty of times when you won't readily have answers to questions that may arise. Having books and various trade magazines at your disposal gives you the opportunity to locate the answers you need, providing quick resolutions. Reading transforms your mind. The more you read, the more you will believe. If you're constantly hearing the same things over and over, eventually, you will start to believe them.

A lot of times when you are pursuing your passion, mentors may be hard to locate. Reading provides some of the best mentorship opportunities from some of the greatest people who ever lived. In most cases, highly successful people do not have the time to literally sit down and mentor you one on one. However, they will put their knowledge in a book. If you are just willing to go to your nearest library, you will be able to find the information you need to push you toward success.

We are living in an age where information is king. If you possess the right knowledge and information, people will pay you lots of money just to know what you know. Always remember, your value in the lives of others is measured by the amount of knowledge you possess. I encourage you to challenge yourself to read at least one book a month. I promise your thinking will begin to dramatically change.

Begin to think of a plan you can use to challenge yourself in reading. Start by thinking of an accountability partner and allow them to hold you to the standard of reading at least one book a month.

_____

_____

_____

_____

_____

_____

_____

_____

_____

_____

_____

_____

_____

_____

_____

10 Chapter Ten

OVERCOMING FEAR

When I was about nine years old, I was a member of the local Boys and Girls Club. I was fortunate enough to experience a multitude of things that provided me with valuable lessons on life. I remember when I wanted to learn how to swim. There was no way for me to ever get the proper training I needed until I decided to jump in the pool. At the time, two of my brothers were there with me; my older brother, who already knew how to swim in the deep end, and my younger brother who couldn't swim either.

Although I didn't know how to swim, I decided to consult with both of my brothers before taking my crash course in swimming. Immediately my older brother said, "Man go ahead and jump in. It's not as bad as you think. There is only one way to figure out if you have what it takes to swim in the deep end. If you jump in and can't survive, don't worry I'll jump in and save you." My younger brother, on the other hand, decided to chime in and give his two cents worth of advice, being quick to disagree with everything my older brother told me. "Don't do it man! You can't swim, so how do you expect to swim in the deep end and you haven't learned how to swim in the shallow end. That's crazy! If you do this, I'm telling Momma as soon as we get home."

At that very moment, I was confronted with a very hard decision. I could make the jump into the deep end and possibly experience the greatest level of joy imaginable for me at the time; or I could choose not to jump and go home another day, wondering what would have happened if I decided to take the risk. Also, I was thinking about whether or not it was worth the whipping I could potentially get when I got home.

Immediately, I closed my eyes and heard my heart beating as loud as a bass drum. My palms were sweating because of the anxiety and I jumped into the middle of the deep end. Suddenly, I felt the cool refreshing water hit my body. I opened my eyes underneath the water and began to panic, fluttering my arms and legs, in hopes to start heading back toward the top of the pool. It worked! I finally had control of the situation. I popped my head out of the water, and looked over at my brothers with a big smile. I began to shout and swam to the edge of the pool to get out. From that moment on, I knew how to swim and I was extremely excited about the freedom I received by doing something new.

While aggressively pursuing your passion, there will be times you will have to make decisions in the middle of being fearful. You will never fully know how something will turn out until you fully engage in it. Whatever level of success you're seeking will require you to move past fear. By doing this, you too will experience the greatest joy you've ever known. I promise you, it's worth the risk.

Think about some of the fears that keep you from stepping into your dreams and goals. Now write down how you are going to press pass these fears and practice being an overcomer.

_____

_____

_____

_____

_____

_____

_____

_____

_____

_____

_____

_____

_____

_____

_____

_____

_____

_____

_____

_____

_____

_____

_____

_____

_____

_____

_____

_____

_____

_____

_____

_____

_____

_____

11 Chapter Eleven

IN CONCLUSION

In conclusion, I want to express the importance of living your life to the fullest. If you look as far as your next door neighbor's house, you will see a world full of unfulfilled people who are seeking to do more than just the norm. I hope by reading this book, you decide to no longer be ordinary.

Imagine how you would feel if you knew what it was you wanted and you accomplished it? Have you ever wondered how it felt to win in everything you set out to do? Guess what, everyone does. If it were easy, no one would be searching for happiness and fulfillment. It takes a special person to desire something more and have faith to take action. I believe you are that person! You are not normal; in fact, you are uniquely designed to be someone great in the earth. The one thing I want you to always remember is to follow your passion. Our world would have less crime and drug infested communities if people were to follow their dreams. The reason some people die young doing something illegal is due to them constantly feeling like a failure.

We all have fears and struggles that try to keep us from becoming successful. However, we must build up our minds to become mentally strong enough to handle the challenges in life. I can't promise you that your journey will be easy. What I can promise is if you desire to do something great, your life will be fulfilled in such a way that you could have never imagined.

If this book has sparked a flame in you to pursue your dreams, so you can live your life to the fullest without any regrets, let me know. I'd love to hear from you. Write me to express your thoughts.

Dr. Gabriel E. Warren
P. O. Box 361391
Birmingham, AL 35236
www.gabrielewarren.com
www.facebook.com/DrGabrielWarren

ABOUT THE AUTHOR

Dr. Warren is a seasoned business-man, educator, author, and entrepreneur. He is the co-founder and president of OneKiss Inc., a nonprofit organization whose mission is to educate, mentor, and coach married couples. In addition to his presidential duties, Dr. Warren is a business instructor, author of the book titled *No Regrets*, 2008, motivational speaker, and subject matter expert on the topic small business sustainability. He serves as a consultant to new and existing business owners seeking to achieve long-term sustainability.

Dr. Warren has served as a contributing guest writer for online blogs and newspapers, writing inspirational columns focused on marriage and relationships, small business, and motivating individuals to accomplish their goals.

A native of Phenix City, AL, Dr. Warren received his Bachelor of Science degree from The University of Alabama in Tuscaloosa, AL. He holds a Master of Business Administration degree from Ashford University, and a Doctorate of Business Administration degree from Walden University.

He is married to Ebony, and they now have two sons, Gabriel II and Christian, who all reside in Birmingham, AL.